John Urbancik

Mind Chaos

For more information, please visit www.darkfluidity.com

ISBN: 978-1-951522-24-7

JOHN URBANCIK

MIND CHAOS

The wound
is not fresh,
not wet,
almost invisible,
yet still
sometimes
it itches.

The years pile up behind me and I do the best I can, I be me as best I can, I live the life closest to the one I always thought I wanted. And even if the particulars of what I want have changed, it feels like the dream remains the dream, and the dream remains out of reach. How much further is it? How do I get there when every path has led me astray, or toward false victories, toward utter defeat?

I remain defiant, even when I'm forced to step back and start over in another place, another time, another direction.

One of these damn doors is the right one.

Here, I had a story of a wolf. But I've been told, without room for disagreement or even discussion, the wolf must wait.

I do not believe wolves like to wait.

Is the
wolf
an agent
of the
Moon?

Wolves,
like wizards,
know more
than they
reveal.

If the wolf
howls
in your
night,
it is not
alone
and they
have you
surrounded.

Fear—or take comfort.

The path to Midnight...
ah,
but what can I say?
You run
you hide
you slip
you fall
You make the wrong turn
at the wrong time
then welcome,
one and all!
But the path from Midnight
is naught but tears
and maybe death,
but judging by the crows,
maybe not even that.

VELOCITY

the universe is
constantly in motion.

the earth is never twice
in the same space

the planet is a ship
hurtling seemingly out of control
through a vast void
filled with
everything

mathematical vectors
calculating Gravity

the earth is a ship
which feeds us
nourishes us
keeps us
and
protects us

Scars
are natural tattoos

Scars and tattoos
tell their tales
of who we were,
and hint at
who we are,
and act as a compass
to guide us to
who we will be.

DRAGON

Dragons
are creatures
of fire
or of ice,
or of acid
or of death.

THE FOUR BEAUTIES

Beauty should be
revered.

All things and all people
are capable of great beauty.

Some people are convinced
this is not true, that they
have no beauty.

Some people embrace
their ugliness instead.

Beauty
is in
the eye of
the beholder.
Be the beholder
who beholds
beauty.

Every age has its beauty.

REVISIONS

are never
fully and completely
done.

There's always something
that can be changed, fixed,
or made better—every
time you open it, every
time you read it.
Revisions are only done
because we, as authors,
have decided
they are done
enough.

Shaping them
getting the words right
Sculpting them
Refining them

What is right
is easily
subjective
because
it's not
merely what
is correct.

"He suffers the moon sickness."

Sanity
affected by
the phases of the moon

MOON SICKNESS
the moon
influences
fevers

of unsound mind

non compos mentis

I have always believed in the moon.
I have often seen her in the sky
looking down on me.

LUNACY

Do not
trust
the moon
when she
lies.

Beware the dancer
under the moon
for she
might
bring
great
joy

Poetry in motion.
Keep the blood in motion.
Inertia is a state of mind
and a fallacy.
All things are
constantly in
motion.

MOTION

Motion Pictures
an illusion
reinforced
with a
soundtrack

Mechanical
motion
of the
clockworks
men.

the motion
of the
minute hand

Exercise if a form of
physical motion.
Writing is a form of
intellectual and creative motion.

RISK COURAGE

Are you brave enough
to risk everything on a
dream?

DANGER
is ever
present.
You can hide
from it
or embrace it.

You may fear it,
but never
be controlled
by your fear.

the
greatest
most terrible
Risk
is in not
taking
Risks.

Physical
Emotional
Intellectual
Not all risks are identical,
except in the results.
Win or Lose. But, without
risk, there is only Losing

Modern society has reached a place where making money is more important than making things. Art. Manufacturing. Instead, people are taught to invest. If you invest enough money, you can leverage the sweat equity and the things that are made because of it. But if you haven't got enough money, you will continue to spend effort and energy, renting it out for a pittance, so that someone else who did have enough money can make more while you only make enough to pay your rent and further enrich the same people who are underpaying you and getting richer off your labor.

MONEY

But the choice in this world as it is, is to either enter the game and make enough money to live without the structure of rules you didn't write and that don't benefit you, or don't and die.

My shirt was
made with
the silk
of a single
spider.
She was busy.

And I considered,
for a while,
the shape
and textures
of grace.

"I am not a sufficient meal for
you," the man says to the tiger.

The tiger considers this, then says,
"An insufficient meal is better
than no meal at all."

When
the horn
is blown
to signal
the hunt,
hope you are not
the prey.

Consistency is vital when making a comparison. If you count how many oranges are in a bowl of fruit one day, take one away, and the next day count how many fruits in the bowl are not apples—the number of oranges did not go up (necessarily) because, I don't know, the pears?

SEER: "You are on a
journey."
MAN: "We're in a damn
train depot. Of
course I'm on a
journey."

Death is an alchemical reaction.

The adventure is not
going
to the
carnival,
but going
with
the carnival.

RAVENOUS
like
RAVENS
"Feed 'em to the birds."

Of course she carries an Emergency Red Lipstick.

If aliens
planted
the pyramids,
what is
growing
inside
them?

Muted around the edges
by choice,
but it's a bad choice
and you know it.
Bits of your soul
eroding
at the numb edges.
The things you didn't notice.
The colors.
The music.
The people.
Always struggling
to not lose yourself,
but always losing
just a little bit,
a moment here,
a moment there,
until.

"You've managed to elude
capture all this time."

"Well, I am an elusive
bastard."

get out
get away
get lost
get better

the city
the Angels
forgot.

Do you
have
an
Escape
Plan?

I didn't know what would or even might happen. I was a kid. In my experience, spellwork and Ouija boards were made by Parker Brothers. And in all fairness to the thirteen year old version of me, they appeared to be just an ordinary deck of playing cards. I dealt out a Ten of Hearts, a Queen of Diamonds, a King of Clovers, an Ace of Spades. I wasn't working on a royal flush, just a straight. But the last card was a Rogue of Swords, and that's when all the trouble began.

Silver Lake was named for the color of the sliver moon reflecting on its surface on a brisk winter night. The Wolves of the Winter howled in the distance and we made camp in sight of the shore. We knew about the wolves, had been running from the wolves and defending ourselves from the wolves since the White Season fell upon us. The surface of Silver Lake looked wet though it was thoroughly frozen, but we didn't dare risk it under the pale moonlight. We didn't know what was under that icy surface. We didn't know it was hungry. As I said, we only knew the wolves.

She was a pro. Worked the Vegas circuit. So when she dealt out the cards, everyone knew the odds were stacked in her favor. Everyone knew, but the thing of it was—she was beautiful and dangerous and alluring and smart, so nobody cared. The house always won, and every last damned one of them believed they might curry her favor. In the end, even I thought it, or at least hoped for it—it not her true favor, if not her love or devotion or admiration, at least a credible facsimile of it. That's what she sold, what she traded, what she dealt in—masks.

Year 9

The city's still on fire. No idea what's fueling those flames. Never been that close. I assume some variation of sulfur and honest hellfire. At night, it lights all the clouds orange and red. And there are always clouds because they're actually smoke. It's cold in mid-summer now because we haven't seen the sun since Zero Hour.

The car's gassed up, the ammo is hot and heavy and anxious to eat some flesh. I'm going hunting.

For Hell and Glory.

Those who fight cancer and its symptoms, who face the torment of a body in revolt, no matter the type and regardless of its recessions, who bravely fight or gracefully cede, who deal with the pain—they are heroes of the grandest sort, and when death inevitably finds all of us—these heroes will be escorted to Valhalla. To believe anything less is to lack understanding.

MURDER ON THE ORIENT ROCKET SHIP

On the rocket ship, there's no room for conflict. There's no room for water, where the hell are you going to store angst and resentment? Yet here we are, half a galaxy away from earth, with one dead crewman and six suspects.

COLLECTIONS

We collected our collections—cards, dice, comics, hearts—and surrendered them to our new overlords. They laughed as us, mostly, but wanted to know just which of us had been keeping the hearts of our enemies in mason jars.

In the silence
the echoing silence
listening only to my own thoughts
bouncing around
behind my eyes.

the ghosts of Midnight
are active
and noisy
sometimes,
they also walk
like whispers
and speak
in shadow
and watch
every
sin
you
make.

WIND

In Greek mythology,
the winds are gods.
The children of gods.
Powers onto themselves.

Today, we have hurricanes.

Are hurricanes the maddest,
least sane of the winds?
Or the most dedicated?

In my stories, the wind is almost always a woman, even a girl, young but not necessarily naïve. I personify wind perhaps as much as the moon.

Perhaps, but not quite.

the wind
tells
secrets
because
everyone
tells
the wind.

Is this wind always a wild thing?
Yes.

All of us write for different reasons. For deadlines. For our fans. For our friends. But all of us started in the same place. We had a story to tell and a means by which to tell it. None of us were any good, not at the start. We didn't know how to string sentences together. We didn't know what to include and what to leave out. We didn't know what had already been done before. Any sophistication our first stories had was all in our heads. But if we discovered we had more stories to tell, more sentences to string together, then we didn't stop. Hopefully, we never lose that initial motivation: we have a story to tell and the means by which to tell it.

MOTIVATION

Spare a few coppers?

Inserted into the slot of an old automaton. The gears click as they turn, and a prize is distributed.

IN WHOM WE TRUST

An old coin
from a distant land
traded for a favor
yet to be named.

A coin marked
with the head
of a dragon.
Forged by a dragon.

After the last prize is given,
the next win will grant
the automaton motion,
if not life.

A coin marked with the face of a jaguar.

A new coin
from a private mint
stolen in anticipation
of a favor to be named
later.

AIRPLANE

A steel shell propelled
across great distances
at tremendous heights.

On a flight from one place you know
to another, unknown place
existing in a different time,
where they speak another language,
you become the Outsider
you always feared.

PAPER AIRPLANES

the airplane
of the future,
now it's
the airplane
of the past.

Face of the clock is astronomical and alchemical iconography.

Soldiers
of Time

There are stories, so many stories, that aren't mine to tell. But I'd send you to them, to the places where you'll hear them, because you need to know about these stories.

ENGRAVED

The sound of drums, of marching feet,
of a clock ticking away until death.

Terrible times
require terrible
sacrifice.

Time tells stories.

The man with the knife knows the importance of time. He waits until the time is perfect, then sets to cutting. Not before.

The first story is of a man versus nature, possibly a cat, possibly a storm. The second story is a romance with complications.

I'll trade you one thousand words for a picture.

ATLAS

MAP

Even
after set
down on a
map, the
course of
the river
will change.
Time refuses to allow
the river to rest.
We shouldn't rest either.

CARTOGRAPHY

Does the procession of a map tell a story, not just of perception but of history? I have an atlas with Czechoslovakia, East Germany, and the USSR. Where are they now?

Once upon a time
no one knew where
a road might take
you, not even the
road itself. Then
man came along with
their maps and said
this road goes only
to this place.
But the maps lie.
And change.
And the roads
have minds of
their own.

JOHN URBANCIK

GRAVEYARD

Do they bury
their dead
out of respect
or fear?

Always, the dead
are rising. Eating.
Killing. Better to
burn the corpses
and scatter the ashes
and be done
with them entirely.
The soul is separated
at the cessation of life.

CODE
CODE
CODE
CODE
CODE
ODE
DE
E

what if you
break the code
and it says, breaking
the code will end the world
You wouldn't believe it. But if
the world suddenly came to an end,
it really would be all your fault, wouldn't it?
No. Who put such
power in a code
and locked it?
what if
that was
also you?

Written in code. Backwards in a foreign language. With irrelevant words added. What if the irrelevant words are an entire secondary secret message?

Cracking
the code
really requires
recognizing
patterns.

CRYPTOGRAPHER

POINT OF VIEW is vitally important in a work of fiction. It may tell us who the main character is or who we should listen to, but it also provides structure and limitation. We know only this and no more. Point of View is a fundamental architectural characteristic in the construction of any tale.

PERSPECTIVE

Observation
is a function
of your vantage.

Looking up at
something
is not the same as
looking down.

What you see matters.
Where you see it from
also matters.

VANISHING POINT
the endless infinite
recedes to a singular point.
A singularity?
A black hole?

Spellcasting in the old style is rare anymore. Today, you mostly find illusionists playing at magic or conjurers pretending at necromancy when instead their skills lie in pulleys and ropes and smokes and ventriloquism. A true artiste is difficult to find. Not impossible. Merely difficult—and probably dangerous.

MAGIC

Magician, disappear thyself!

You create flowers
from nothing
and levitate
sleeping beauties.
Then you open doors
and call down
the lightning
and raise the dead
from their tombs.
And I need
your help,
magician.

A traveling magician brings tricks to amaze and delight, but also promises of deeper, heavier, more consequential things that cannot properly be called tricks.

Is the illusionist some sort of human embodiment of a trickster you?

Once more,
I'll let loose
with one last tear.

I've never sat
beneath a vanilla orchid
before.

I wonder
if she's
wondering
anything.

One last flight
out of paradise
before it's
locked down
and we're
trapped
forever.

VISION
The sense of sight.
Also:
the ability to see
beyond that which you see.

It can be
said of a man,
even a man who
is blind, that
he has great
vision.

Visions of the Future

A Vision in Red

Vision
is a synonym for beauty.
She is a vision.

do not get lost in the glow of the night

Because
her eyes—
they'll trap you
and keep you.

at night
under
moonlight
they whisper
of a legend

...the amount of light
necessary
to light up
the palace.

two
lovers
approach
en Tango

Have I got
a story
to tell you?
You bet
I do!

all this
happened
more or less.

I've written poetry
before,
she tells me,
but then she
whispers
secret
poetics
through her eyes.

In the willow's shade
I dream
and in my dreams
I am beautiful.
And so are you.

Today
it rained.
It came
down in
ceaseless
torrents,
washing
away all
the fears
and all
the hopes,
wiping
everything
clean
for a
fresh
start,
if you
want it.

Hurricane force winds
change the landscape
but not the way
I feel.

You are
my favorite
storm.

Sometimes
my fingers
just need
to be
scribbling
words.
Such nonsense
as has never
been tested.

Do you know what's going on here?
I don't.
I don't even have a guess.
I assume it's all just
dreams within dreams.

DELICAT DELERIA
when
your
world
fractures

how
much
ink
have
you
got?

ONE
DROP
OF
INK
AT
A
TIME

We will not repeat the same catastrophe.

Sometimes it's a word, just a word, a series of them scratched out onto wood pulp, until they either make some sort of sense or not—sometimes it's just a series of words arranged in a particular order that allows for the breath of life in a character or a place or a story—sometimes it's just a series of short little words strung together in such a way as to change lives.

Is this the shadow version
of the world?
Does that mean the shadow version
of me is in my world?

If I had a story to tell, would you listen? Would you pay attention? Would you ask the questions that need to be asked? Poke holes in the plot? Suspect the motives of the characters? Would you understand my purpose, my point, my intention—or would you write me off as crazy?

What if our world
is actually
the dark side
of the
shadow world?

I made cookies, chocolate chip of course, intending to bring them to the party—the same party that last year ended with Donna playing Blind Man's Bluff with Jack, which no one expected—but I forgot to add vanilla, which I had gotten shipped special from Madagascar specifically to make these cookies, so I ended up having a very full cookie jar where never before there had been a cookie jar, which I picked up while getting additional chocolate chips for the second batch, and I only just realized I am completely out of eggs for tomorrow's breakfast.

EVENSONG

Did you say
you made plans?
Have you learned
nothing?

A turn of phrase
like a twist of the knife
and it's over.

Waking in the middle of the early morning halfway between midnight and dawn, you find the worst of the thoughts have clamored out of the deepest wells to crowd your head with stupid ideas.

The dreams continue.

Some nights, I am spared the endless ceaseless relentless push and pull of dreamtide. The damage isn't always permanent, much like dreams, but it changes me, forces me to grow or retreat.

Retreat is always easier in the immediate. In the now. It's always costlier, in the long run. In the uncounted tomorrows. I pay for every unconscious retreat, every moment in which I embraced my invisibility, every voice I listened to that was not my own.

Or yours. I should have listened more to—not to your words, but to your tone, your emotions, your intentions.

I've known a long time now that you loved me—and that I loved you.

But love isn't always brave, so maybe it took too long to admit it.

I've wanted to be brave. I've attempted it. I promised open, honest, and forthright from the start, when the secrets hadn't yet formed.

Even then, the secrets knew, when you didn't know and when I didn't know, the secrets knew how to find us, the shapes of two of us then already beginning to form the single shape of us now.

Dreams are funny things. I want more control over them. I want my dreams to bring me closer to you when I can't be physically close. I want to hear your voice and feel your breath and hold your hand as we walk the streets of faraway cities.

Instead, I dream of drowning. Wave after wave of water—but not in waves, in horizontal lines so I have to gulp air in the lines between the water lines.

Do I drown in the absence of you? I never thought so before. Something has changed. Something vital—inside me, inside us.

I don't want to find you in my dreams. I lied to you and to myself. I want, when I dream of drowning, to wake from those dreams and find you in my waking.

In the full light of the sun, I dream about the dreams I might find when I close my eyes. I want to kiss you in my dreams, to walk with you, to hold your hand—but most nights, you elude me. I can't control my dreams as well as I would like, so I go whole nights, sometimes a week of nights or more, wherein I dream things other than you. This isn't to say I don't appreciate the images, the scenarios, even the people I might find in those dreams. But while you are distant, while you are away from me, breathing different air and eating different food, I should at least be able to see you in my sleep. I risk madness or something worse if I can only see you in the dreams I dream when I'm awake.

Trial by Tears
Your worst moments
repeated
until you cry
and die,
and we all
get to watch.

An overseas phone call,
a voice with an accent
and shared memories,
a reminder of things lost.
It doesn't matter
if you answer it,
the tears glisten freshly
within your eyes.

What skills
do you bring
to bear?

Eloquence
does not equate to
certainty.
It just
sounds good.

Dragonfire
and emeralds:
a festive
combination
in winter.

I need a distraction.

It's just you
and the darkness
until the sun crawls
up from the abyss.

The morning after
you wake alone
and wonder
how it all went
so wrong
and yet also
so right.

dance
if you
want

You were never meant
to be alone.
You will always
Be haunted.

Do all the things
with all your passion.

The line to get in
as midnight approaches
stretches all the way
around the building.
Inside, the music throbs
and strangers crowd
the dance floor
but it's only
a place of waiting
before moving on
to Hell or Heaven.
It's not how you lived
or what you did,
it's not the skills you bring
or the money you've got,
it's all about
how hard you dance.

My past haunts my dreams. Never directly. Always in roundabout ways I've got to work to interpret. Past insecurities, past losses, past heartbreak come echoing back at me, all relentless and without mercy.

But there's been a change. Not a fundamental change. Not an overhaul of the nature of my dreams, generally. But once or twice, I dream of the future, a possible future, in which you and I are united against the demons, shadows, and ghosts of both our pasts. I'm stronger with you, you're stronger with me, and maybe our combined power—you and me together—is more than you and me combined but separated—maybe it will be enough.

What exactly would enough look like? I haven't got a clue, not a real one, but I've seen hints of it in dreams when you hold my hand, when you kiss me, when you whisper.

I think, if I give it any real thought, I think enough looks like you and me. Enough looks like lazy days, your head on my shoulder, your hand on my chest, my arm around you. We could have wine or whiskey or tequila. We could talk or dance or run our fingers over each other, it doesn't matter, because this is and always will be the definition of enough. More than enough. An abundance. Maybe not an inexhaustible supply—that might be naïve to believe—but endlessly replenishable.

Dreams can be shattered. The memories of possible futures, the echoes of the past, reduced to shards.

And you're expected to clean up, though every piece cuts you, some just the slivers that can kill you in their thousands, others straight to the bone.

After, sometimes, the dream returns, not with promises but merely a shred of hope. Enough to make it seem worth the effort of forcing broken glass back into place.

It might never be the same. But maybe it can be fortified, strengthened, made into something different but still beautiful.

Laying there, not dreaming, not
sleeping despite the hour, thinking
I've been invisible in your life,
giving you time and space when
what you really needed was grace,
empathy, and love.

I'm sorry for the way I've failed
you—failed us.

The maps of my world, the cities and streets I've lived in and walked on, have changed over time. Places exist in four dimensions. I may know a moment here or there, but I don't know every moment of those places—especially when the world is ever-changing and infinitely mutable.

Give me a moment to remember all that I've intentionally forgotten. I may cry. Just wait. I'm not asking you to deal with the mess you left in me. But I've got to get through a fair amount of pain, anger, frustration, and betrayal before I can find the reasons why I loved you. They're way back there, buried under the detritus of your wreckage and ruin.

the roads around here
twist violently,
rise and fall like kings,
and cling perilously close
on either side
to stone walls
and bottomless chasms
into eternity.

The last thing I expected when I walked into the bar was a standing ovation and three ladies offering whiskey and generous smiles. I looked around for a bit like someone lost and wandering, which is the only way I know how to look around anymore, and eventually I did ask the bartender what was up with all the attention. “Didn’t you know?” she said. “You’re a superstar.”

I spent the night in someone’s home, slept off the whiskey, and made it back to the road by noon.

I’ve crisscrossed the country several times since then, and I’ve looked for that bar and that town, but I’ve never found my way back. Probably, there never had been such a place, not in the real world, and that was the closest I got to being tempted out of this one.

Darkness
and bourbon
are your only
companions
at 3am.

I wandered
into a dream again
and met a man
who promised
secrets and treasures
awaited,
but when I asked
where and when
he said
he wasn't
wise enough
to know.

Nothing
hurts
forever
You won't
live that
long.

A single note
on a violin
echoing through
the vastness
of space,
the limits
of time,
but it's
this one note
that
breaks
your heart
over
and
over
again.

The game isn't
designed to be won,
just to be played
until you have
used up all your love
and exhausted
every ounce of faith.
After the game,
you'll learn if it was worth it.

Ever listen to silence?
True silence?
I can't.
My mind, my ears,
something creates
sound when there is none.
I need music
to sit in silence.
I need your heartbeat
pressed against mine
to know peace.

I hear the
thunder

What did you hear?

what you see
is a matter of
Perception.

Electromagnetic
Spectrum

what
do you
see
when
you
close
your
eyes
and
really
look?

Seeing
is believing
but don't trust your eyes.

Without
clarity of mind
you cannot have
clarity of purpose.

I am
all that
you see
and all
that you
can't.

I see
you

RUMOURS

No one remembers
how it started.
They only
remember
what was said.
Those words persist
and echo,
maybe not until
the end of time,
but at least as far
as the end of
memory.
That's how Rumour
works.

I told myself
a story of you.
I invented you
from nothing
and made you
perfect
before I heard
a rumour
that perhaps
you were real
and telling yourself
stories of me.

There are no facts.
There are no fictions.
There are only Rumours
and Innuendoes.

That's how Rumours
get started.
In a little book.
Words scribbled
on a page.
Lies.
Stories.
Exaggerations.
Fabrications.
That's how Rumours
get started:
when you don't
fill in the truth
and let them
make it up.

I have gathered
all the Rumours
whether they look like truths,
sound like truths,
or are truths.
I have tested
all the secrets
and wondered
at the mysteries,
then plotted it all out
on a map
inevitably
leading
to you.

Tell me a story
as though it
were true.
Tell me a tale
about me
and yes you.
We'll make it
the stuff
of legend.
All legends start
as Rumour.

the Geographer
and
the Astronomer

The Hidden
Heart
of the
City

Game
Of
Empires

He hates carrying keys.
So of course he has to.
A servant of
Sereca.

thread made of mercury

—"You were always
beautiful.
Even with
the scars.
—"And now?"
—"Now I
see how
ugly you
always were."

Who is the hero of this tale?

In a forest kingdom
far from here
of which you may have heard tell
Lived a brave young hero
whom you may know
by the name of Hunter-Belle.

But deep in the bowels
of the close-by mountain
there lived a great beast of old,
a dragon with scales
the deepest of red
breathing fire terribly cold.

So our hero set out,
quicksilver sword in her hand,
to defeat the monster so cruel.
Despite all of the warnings
and all of the fears
she'd remembered in song as a girl

Hunter-Belle faced the dragon
on a long winter night
and their battle was heard far and wide,
but when the ice was cleared
all the townsfolk feared
it was their hope, not the dragon, who died.

Scratched and scorched
but walking straight,
with a grin, or so I've heard tell,
our hero returned,
quicksilver sword in her hand,
and we feasted our own Hunter-Belle.

We shared a
near death
experience.
What did you
expect would
happen next?

You don't have to
know all the answers.
But you should not
stop asking the
questions.

I don't always know the difference between a promise and a threat, but I am making one now.

I wandered another street today and got lost again and discovered an old tavern with a cellar. It was dark down there and well hidden, so it was just me and the rats and a collection of old bottles of bourbon. Smooth stuff. They never even knew I was there.

They think they've got me trapped. And they do, but only physically and not forever. The body will fail one day and they will no longer have me.

Beauty

Give me
a moment,
a chance,
a hope,
even a prayer.
Because
I want
to at least
dream of you
if you'd
allow it.

Elegance

I remain
essentially
unchanged
yet vastly
uncertain.
Unchained
or untethered?
I need you
to tie me down.

In the dark
of midnight
and the light
of the full moon
I can see you,
not directly,
but in the places
left behind
by your absence.

Style

I am
haunted by
the ghost
of me.
Do your
magic.
Anchor me
to here
and now.

I am
"broken"
but I'm not
broken
in the same way
I was
three or four years ago.

The state of
brokenness
is fluid.

Ethereality
of
Touch
something
that doesn't
seem real
when you
touch it.
Floats under
your fingers

EXTRAORDINARY

Your soul
is a phoenix
burnt to ash
over and over
but rising again
in fiery glory.

Streets
of asphalt
and
screaming
metal
and
death.

I can't
love you
more,
yet I do
every
damn
day.

My job
right
now
is to
re-discover
my zen.

All the streetlights
reflecting off
every rain-splattered
surface like
a million fireflies
in the night.

Grief
haunts
with
The
Echoes
of love
lost
in
the
empty
places
left
behind
by their
absence.

I want you
for my sunrise.
And sunset.
And moonrise.

A man
of
dust
and
shadow.

When I was lost
in the darkness,
you didn't try
to pull me from it.
You took my hand
and sat in silence with me.
That meant everything.

Our secret second meeting.
After the
first kiss,
because the
first kiss will
always be the
first, special
and extraordinary
and unforgettable.

In a world
of magic
and myth
comes a man
of science.

It's been a glorious run.
I had hoped for a
magnificent end,
but I suppose
this will do.

Morning arrives unexpectedly, but we deal with it, we rise and face our demons, we scramble our eggs and drink our chocolate, and really, we're unstoppable. Twilight arrives unexpectedly, but we deal with it, and midnight won't be far behind.

Age is evil. It comes when you don't expect it, and the damage it causes will kill you. At 20, you don't anticipate 25. At 30, you can't imagine 40. By 48, you see a path leading from you straight to a grave. There's no change or reprieve. When you're 117, every day is unexpected. How many more breaths must I take? And now they want me to save the world one more time...

Every day, the news gives us something else to be offended by, another injustice or inequity, another slip of the tongue—or other body parts—meant to incite and divide us. Yes, every day, there's something to be angry about. Sometimes, the only thing you can do is turn off the news and say today I haven't got time to be angry.

There are things I don't understand. Some, I pretend to understand and I can get by that way. But sometimes, I just don't understand and I can't fake it.

You can't kill me. I'm the only one who knows how this book is supposed to end.

As the world experiences turmoil at the hands of politicians and corporations...

necklaces and bracelets and earrings and
hair pins holding up an enormous
quantity of hair and a jeweled headpiece
that glitters in the moonlight.

I didn't know who she was or where she came from, but I was ready to assume she was a queen or a goddess and she'd come from another time.

"Are you always acting?" he asked. "Are you acting now?"

"Of course."

"Act like someone who loves me."

"It'll only be an act."

"That's okay," he said. "I'm probably treacherous. And I'm only interested in the sex."

I didn't know
there would be
a jazz band

Another night to forget,
another glass of whiskey,
another cheap blonde or redhead.
It never changes.
Memory just doesn't give up
on something perfect.

A big fat
yellow moon
hung low
on the
edge of
the field.

Beware
the Man
with the
Silver
Eye

On the subway, I noticed all the stained glass at every stop in Brooklyn.

I'm not fit to determine what it means, except to say I didn't see a single broken panel. And I have to think the people who put the glass in, and the people who proposed it and approved it, did so with confidence.

And I have to think that's a good thing.

Together
we can be
phantoms
happy in love
and inspiring
all the best
stories

I saw
an image
of you,
your poetic
soul
shining
through
the sepia
of years
long gone,
and I wish
you could be
my ghost lover.
We could walk
hand in hand,
the feather touch
of your fingers,
the honey
of your voice
reciting poems
straight
from your soul,
and a first kiss
guaranteed
to send shivers
through my bones

Let's haunt
the old castle
together,
walk upon
those cold
stone floors,
spook the royals,
dance in the ballroom,
streak our fingers
in the mirrors,
howl at the moon
with the wolves,
and on a certain night
once every year,
when the barriers
are soft
and we
are made flesh
if only
for a little while,
let's make
full use
of our flesh
and inspire
each other
to scream.

the Saint of Seventh Street

Trouble ordering
hot chocolate
today because
pronunciation.
Hot chocolate has
a skin on it,
like pudding,
and it's so
incredibly thick
it coats your
mouth and
your soul
and for a moment
at least,
everything
everywhere
is good.

When you speak
with someone who
doesn't know your
language, it's easy to
misinterpret their inability
to articulate as an inability
to think cohesively. But you
are just as incapable of speech
in their language, and nothing
will reinforce that so greatly and
completely as moving to another
country which does not
speak your language.

Having settled myself with a mid-afternoon chocolate crema—don't judge, I'm still suffering the journey and the jetlag—I'll walk through the park for a bit and maybe eat something, if the mood strikes. But which park? I live on a hill. No matter where I go, I'm going uphill for half the journey.

A stranger
wandering
in the silence of
not knowing.

Outside the edge of the shadows, exposed to the sun in all his vibrant and horrible glory, teased by the spray of fountain water in the wind. Boys doing tricks with their soccer balls, girls laughing on their phones, couples walking, music playing, and all around us cars and buses on streets but we don't care.

Paper shops everywhere, with notepads and fountain pens and pencils and joys of every type for scribbling and doodling and crafting masterpieces or attempted masterpieces. Not every corner, but almost as common as *fruterias* or *cervecerias.*

But because of where I am, the magic pens will only work their magic in Spanish—*en español*—unless wielded by a true maestro.

Lost
in a sea of words,
the structure of which
are not yet known,
a mystery
in need of
resolution.

Who else lives in the park?
Not all stories
seem to be romances.
A kind of fairy,
not one,
nor even a hundred,
but a thousand or more.
Established:
the line is thinnest as twilight
ravens exist in both places simultaneously
ravens are harbingers or messengers of either good
or wicked intent
carousels

PARK STORIES
fairy tales
and
ghost stories

Once upon a time, a girl was lost there. A child. She wandered somewhere between here and there, seeing and being seen but only sometimes, skipping days or weeks at a time, so that many years passed but only some for her. And now, for reasons unfathomable, it's time for the woman who once was a girl to find her way home again.

Is she angry? Grateful? Resentful? Scared? Murderous? All these things at once?

in some spaces,
  the buildings are
  blocks consisting
  primarily of
  rectangles and squares
  and perhaps,
  at the top,
  triangles.
other spaces
  are filled
  with angles
  and arcs
  and statues
  and flourishes.

Towers. Spires. Minarets. They race along the rooftops, but should perhaps exercise a bit of care.

Even the wind, one time, slipped from a slick rooftop and fell onto a fire escape and sprained her ankle. She passed out from the pain and might have been captured and enslaved.

She was fortunate—then. You might not be.

A land untouched by time,
where age doesn't matter and
history is happening now, you
never know who or what
you'll discover.
It may even be yourself.

Given what we know,
and what we don't know,
it's not a big surprise
when you learn something
entirely new.

What can I tell you?
Only the truth.
Primarily the truth.
Perhaps, as I spin my tales,
I'll incorporate a bit of truth
when you least expect it.

After the tower fell, language was shattered so that brother could not speak with brother, so that mother could not speak with son. Cities were born, and nations next, and armies, and war seemed inevitable. In a last, desperate attempt to avoid the battlefield, they call upon:

the Interpreter.

A stranger arrived in the Palace of the Winds. She came without finery, but she demanded a room and a meal—not a feast, she said, she was merely passing through. So a meal was prepared and a room given, and there was much dancing in the Palace of the Winds that night, and many bottles of wine were successfully navigated, and in the morning the stranger was gone.

But what did she take with her when she left? Perhaps a piece of silver, perhaps a piece of gold, maybe a satin dress the color of sunset. But maybe she took with her a child, yet to be born, of the Prince of the Winds, a child who one day might have a claim on the throne. Perhaps on that day, the court will learn the name of the stranger, and her true, if devious, purpose.

A haunted house.
A werewolf.
A cult.
A ghost.
A demon.
The possibilities are limitlessly dangerous.
It's all about Atmosphere.

do you go in?
do you run away?
do you open the door?

ATMOSPHERICS

If the story feels
like it's all over the
place, that's because
it is. Intentionally.
It's all about
atmosphere. Absurdities.
Possibilities.

He watches her lips as she speaks. He tries to understand, but the words are fast and foreign. He tries to see how they're structured, how her mouth forms the sounds, but he merely falls deeper in love.

She brings beauty from the north, all ice blue eye and black hair thick like the long, long night. When she looks at you, into and through you, she sees every secret shame, every hidden truth, every ounce of untapped strength. So if she loves you, if she loves you even for one night, she is not merely seeking to share warmth, she sees something that makes you worthy.

I believe I've ordered a piece of bread and hot chocolate, but I'm not always right and sometimes I'm surprised. It's like I want to keep myself on my toes, so I order something and sit and wait and let them surprise me. But I think, I believe, I got this one. Let's see.

The bread, a cheese bread, is served warm! So I got it right, yet still I'm surprised. And delighted.

Every building, every bridge and overpass, every archway and alley and park, is a chance for artistic expression, and the artists of Midnight have been busy. Nothing is plain, but so many styles are represented—gothic and art deco and realism and cubism and abstraction—it's not merely eclectic, it's chaotic—gorgeously chaotic and colorful and dark.

is it time
for the
White Raven
to rise
again?

Magic
is
mathematics
and
linguistics

Was Prince
an aspect of
Baron Samedi,
who was associated
with sexuality
and
the color purple?

Have I ever known
a love so grand?
It seems a dream,
a fantasy wrapped
in memory,
a fever
I recovered form
long, long ago.

I thought
I'd lost her
forever
but she was
a shadow
and shadows
never die.

He thought
he was
entitled
because
he was a
godling.

In a
world
of
Wonder
and
Imagination

But
it's
just
a
regular
pen.

A book of spells
starts with
self-realization
self-actualization
self-care
self-love
and the
trimming
and
cutting
of
self-doubt.

I've seen
the flash
in your eyes,
that vibrancy
in the darkness.
I loved it then
and I love it now,
your excitement
as your bare
the broken pieces
of you
and the blood
you spilt,
and I hope
you know
I will clean
your wounds
and bandage them
and kiss
the fresh cuts
until you
don't need
to bleed.

The foundation
of all magic is
imagination.

Dreams
reside
in
halls
of
Crystal.

I'd love
to read
the stories
of you
etched onto
your
skin.

I remember
the faces
of everyone
who's ever
dreamt of me.

Her kisses
can soothe me
to the bone
or burn me up
from the inside.

Streets are made for wandering. They're designed to remove some of the uncertainty. You know this is a place other people have been before you.

Even paths in the woods, even paths made by deer, you know they lead somewhere.

What about the paths in your head? The meandering routes accessible only to you and only when you shut your eyes, shut out all the stimulation from outside of you. They can lead absolutely anywhere. No one's been there before. It's your space, and your space alone.

Can we wander virtual spaces? Scrolling through algorithms to be exposed to pictures and thoughts and sounds and movies we've never seen before?

Even the ads—some ads—show us wondrous new toys, little playthings we not only want but actually can own.

My scrollings will show me artistic paper for origami and poetry, art prints, chess sets, button up shirts, candles in a variety of scents, bronze dice, cameras, women dancing, acrobats defying death, baskets of fruit or flowers, pencils, books, new scientific theories and discoveries, and cats.

You can't get away from the cats. Not even when you're wandering the physical streets of a towering glittering city.

good old-fashioned
gothic romance

YEARNING

Stone steps
spiraling
up the tower
reaching for
your unknown
heart's desire.

Never
lose your memory
of me

Even gods
and godlings
yearn
sometimes.

An image of her
in my head
driving
my every
move

How much
do you dream,
do you wish,
do you hope?
What will you
sacrifice
to fill the hole
in your heart?

I want to descend
with you into the
darkest parts of us
and thrive.

Answer
my dreams,
since
you made me
dream them.

When I see you
my heart
skips a beat—
but if I can't
see you
it will stop.

Time doesn't work that way.
It just keeps moving.

Tick
Tock
time
won't
stop

I feel the loss
of every second
with the beating
of my heart

CLOCK

If the face
of the clock
is a compass rose,
to where does it
lead us?

The face of the clock tells
the secrets, and sometimes
lies to keep them. The bells
chime to illuminate inevitability,
the persistence of motion, the
unfathomable endings that await
us all. Lie to me, clock, if you
must, so I can get through
one more day.

tigers
care not
for clocks

Can we use
the clock
like an atlas
to trek
through time?

dreamscapes

Walk with me
through the valley
of our dreams

did you dream of me?
was it a nightmare
or was it lovely?

Even
waking dreams are
important. Trust your
visions to guide you, but
don't always take them
at their word.

I have this dream in which you and I travel together to mystical and magical adventures until all of time comes to a halt. So don't tempt me with your dreams of romance. I have already fallen.

Nightmares
flourish
when we fear;
Nightmares
evaporate
when we love.

In the mists
of dreamscapes
as yet
unrealized

You should kiss me.
An exchange
of lips
and tongues
and heart
and memory,
an exchange
of thoughts
and emotions,
of intensity
and exploration,
an exchange
of our souls.
A proper introduction
of me to you
and you to me
and a prelude
to what may come.

Bathed in moonlight
and fragrant breezes,
you come to me
at midnight
and fold into
my embrace.
You have tears.
I have tears,
but I smooth
your hair
down your back
and whisper
reassuring sounds
until your trembling
transforms to anticipation.
You seek in my eyes,
all the promises
and warnings,
and press your lips
against mine.
The kiss gives and takes,
shifts with the stars,
takes us to
the first light of dawn
when all that remains
are two entangled roses
that bloom
only in the light
of the moon.

Do you dance
for your money?

Do you beg?
Borrow?
Steal?
Do you give
a piece of
yourself
five (or more)
days a week?

Give me a dollar,
I'll share my dreams.

Trade
with
me.
Emotions.
Kisses.
Promises.
Futures.

COIN

A penny for your thoughts,
once upon a time, was a
nice price. You could buy
a candy with a penny. Then.

the jingle
of coins
spilling
across
the floor
after
you finally
defeat
the bad guy
who was
obviously
hording
them
all this
time.

Artists
should
not
have to
starve.

Dance
as if your heart
requires it.

Bang Bang
the drums
command

Don't expect
simple solutions. This isn't
merely music. It's a way of life, a
blueprint for a greater tomorrow at a
time when most aren't feeling that possibility.

Do
you
hear
the
drums
pounding
through
the
mist?

Can you use
the beat
to understand
the future?

fall out of step

one step
after another
with the drum
as we march
into oblivion

The hammer of the
drums dictates the
pace of your dreams.
Break the rhythm
and forge
your own way.

I want to dream
of you dancing.

LOVE
makes us brave,
leads us to do
all the things
we only dreamt of,
makes us foolish
in some of the best ways.
Don't ignore
the call of Love,
which has many voices
and many languages.

Love lost
cannot always
be reclaimed.

I have known
the greatest loves.
I will discover
other great loves
if I stay true
and honest
and brave.

love
courage
caring
support
encouragement
trust
beauty

A Mood of Absurdity

the nature
of everything
makes Reality
hard to bare.
While there may be
many escapes
and distractions,
why not choose
Absurdity?

AGENTS OF CHAOS

Do you
believe
in something
unseen?
Something
unknowable?
Something
that defies
reason?

AGENTS OF MISCHIEF

the geometries
get tricky,
angles slide,
voices carry,
intentions
are forgotten,
the mists
consume us.

DARKNESS

Let me
be the candle
that brings
warmth
and comfort
while you traverse
unspeakable darkness.
I have been there,
deep in its grip,
and I survived.
I can't guide you,
but I can
walk beside you.

Darkness
requires
Balance.
Embrace
your
Shadow.

There is always
a light
at the end
of the tunnel—
even if
you can't see it.
Keep going.

MOTION

The ghost
of me
as I
once was
has moved on.
He is me.
I am not him.

Motion in the cyber-age
is e-motion,
which I think
we all know
means love.

POETRY
IN
MOTION

Did you move
too far
too fast
or make
the more common mistake
and not move
fast enough?

Run.
Run if you must.
Find the truest
version of you.
You're out there,
within your chest,
your heart, your soul.

Objects in motion stay in motion, so don't forever sit. Get outside, feel the grass, walk the streets of some other city, swim with dolphins, jump out of an airplane. Whatever you do, do not stop.

In a shop on a corner in some faraway city, I find hot chocolate, break out a special notepad put aside just for this occasion, and wield a fountain pen to craft a spell of beauty—in form and in function—with elegance and grace and style. This isn't a spell of malevolence, and it isn't meant to persuade a change in your behavior, but if I'm successful it will enlighten you to the beauty of you, it will show you what I see when I look into your eyes, it will break the chains that bind you and release your fully articulated spirit into the universe.

Then maybe you'll choose me.

When she closes her fists, she sees the power emanating from them like smoke.

NIGHT

In the night
we believe
the darkness
shrouds
our secrets
and we can
remove
our masks.

Under cover of darkness, witnessed only sometimes by the moon, we shed the skins we wear by day and unleash our truest selves. We dance and howl in smoky clubs driven by gothic rhythms. We learn secrets about ourselves, about our friends, about strangers who are going to be super important in our lives for only this one night. They will unhinge us and release us and transform us into our next magnificent selves.

Dance with me
in the night
in the moonlight
with the stars
and the wolves.
Show me
your truest self
and make me
reveal mine.

He lights a candle.
He thinks the glow might save him. But the danger has already got him in its grasp.
He looks at her, those green eyes so fucking deep, and he knows he's already fallen.
The danger is beautiful. The candlelight reveals a future he didn't think was possible anymore.
He doesn't realize she feels the same danger in the same way.
He doesn't know their adventure, wherever it leads, will be magnificent.

Are you a
Legend?
Do you want
to be?

The lightning bolt gets a quick view of the world and makes rash decisions.

guiding
yourself
through the mindscape
with a machete
and half a dream
and maybe
a touch of hope.

It ain't over yet.
So get back
on your feet,
close your fists,
and fight.

is
it
counting
down
to the
end
or to the
start?

Dreams
of greenery,
of courtyards
escaping
the confines
of this
liminal space,
of birds
and worms
and lightning bugs
and fresh air.

be
alone
with me.

In an old jewelry case, nestled between necklaces and gold rings, she finds an amulet that sinks into her skin and gives her Sight.

How far
would you go
to see
what I see?

A lesson
in history,
linguistics,
and
symbology
unlocks
doorways
to other
dimensions.

Break out.

Not of our dimension, so it can barely be seen, can barely be heard, can barely touch the things we can touch. Yet for too long, it has felt lonely.

A car like a demon
racing from the past
to whatever's next
with reckless abandon.

Action:
Non-stop
and breathless.

A future version of me sent past me a warning. Ten years too late, I found it again—and now I understand. But can I re-work it so I always understood?

Give me
your heart
for my
collection.

Chapter X
Fields of Forges

in which our heroes
must make a mistake
or suffer the consequences.

The Witch
and
the Woodpecker

Three Bears
in the City

FAIRY TALES

Snow Sparrow
just because I've written
one story with a snow
sparrow doesn't mean there
isn't another story to tell.

The Key,
the Pendant,
and the
Jewelry Box

The Night Train

Lessons
for the next
generation
to forget
and ignore.

In the right hands, it's a magic pen and can be made to drop extraordinary shapes in ink.

In the right hands, the magic pen can be a weapon of defense, a means of self-preservation and, quite possibly, salvation.

This is a story of the magic pen
in dreadfully wrong hands.

the
tiger
transformed

Shc's
a spellcaster
and
she will
win my heart
if she wants it.

The Alchemist
works with symbols
and minerals
and esoteric linguistics.

If you don't
believe in magic,
why are you
reading
my spells?

A spell for happiness:
mix ingredients
like flour
and sugar
and brown sugar
with butter,
break some eggs,
add a few
extra teaspoons
of vanilla
and twice as many
chocolate chips
as you think
the cookies need.

is cooking
a form
of alchemy?

Add a little fire
and transform
the ingredients
into something
delicious.

In the woods,
in a secluded house,
he cooks a feast
for guests
he means to impress.
But when
will anyone
show up?
The invitations
went out
long ago.

She draws cards, lays them across the map, then consults shadows within her mind. She radiates a dark, enigmatic mystery, and he is as enraptured by her perfect sharp nails and the texture of red on her lips as by the warnings she's trying to give him.

The moon watches. The moon always watches. Agents of the moon—on the moon, depending on who's telling the story—use telescopes and GPS trackers and a network of finely (not nicely) paid informants. The moon watches. The moon knows.

A council of owls assemble within the skeletal remains of an old barn. They talk about you and they talk about me, and I'm fairly sure this kind of gossip has no place in what should be a fairy tale.

The magician stepped out of the light and disappears forever—taking with him seven expensive watches, eleven wallets, a money clip filled with hundred dollar bills, and one heart.

She's armed with lipstick and other glamours, and she intends to trace him back to his lair.

She's got a special blade for the job.

An army of creatures rise from the sewers. Small creatures that can sneak into everywhere. They rise, and they keep rising, and they forget about us because of infighting.

Most of us, for what it's worth, don't even notice, except maybe to call pest control.

The rift in the Triangle never closed. We just got better at avoiding it.

It's pinpointed to precise coordinates and not as close to Bermuda as you might think.

What the stories don't tell you is that, every time something of ours goes in, something of theirs comes out.

I've never been to Havana.
Not the one in Cuba.
But there's a woman
waiting there for me—
and I don't trust her intentions.

He sought adventure. Romance. Treasure. He watched all the movies, styled himself after his favorite heroes, even made a big deal about finding some bones made of crystal. He claims they almost cost him his life. In truth, it cost him a pack of cigarettes and a pouch of chewing gum.

The musician arrives ready to play. Someone in the audience has a different idea. But when they're later trapped on a plane about to crash in the Himalayas, will they each find the love that has always eluded them?

She wields the sword
with savagery
rarely seen
and cuts down
the serpentine monsters
as quickly as they come.
They cannot
number more than
ten thousand,
and nothing else
stands between her
and her lover
whom they hold
in a subterranean cavern.

EXTRAORDINARY

There are words
that defy
easy explanation.

You are like diamonds,
sharp, laser-focused,
and precious.

You make
doing
the impossible
seem
ordinary.
Which is
utterly
amazing.

I would follow you
but I won't
chase you
unless you ask.

Dance
with me
in the shadows
of Prague
and I'll kiss you
on the Charles Bridge
in the hour
before
we meet
the witch.

I don't know
the stories.
Let's make
one of our own.

I come from Prague, among other places, several generations back. The magic of that city runs through my veins. The architecture is in my bones. Its history is my history.

It's a magic city. Not the only magic city, certainly not, but it's the one with the magic most resonant with my own.

And I was born in New York City!

The shadows of Prague echo in the shadows of me. The music will make me dance. The bars will make me drink. The mysteries will live through me.

Can we haunt
haunted streets
together
like it's our
Destiny?

ACKNOWLEDGMENTS

Thanks, first, to Lunadelarosa, whose encouragement motivated me to rush into this project when I really shouldn't have.

To all my First and Last Readers, people like Amy, Gina, Kya, Karen, and Miko, without whom my words would fall hollow from my head and fingers.

To the Horsemen, with whom I've ridden from the start: Brian, Mike, Mikey, and Coop. You'll never find the bodies in our wake.

To everyone who has ever inspired a stray thought, idea, concept, or color. It all gets churned into something in my head and sometimes becomes something incredible. But not always.

As always, Sabine and the Rose Fairy continue to inspire. I wouldn't even be here if not for them.

ABOUT THE AUTHOR

John Urbancik lives in his mind far more than is probably good for a person. The paths within have led him to places like *Sins of Blood and Stone*, his first novel, the series *DarkWalker*, and his City of Night, Midnight. He hosted a podcast called *InkStains* and may one day do something similar again.

He was born on a small island in the northeast United States called Manhattan, has lived in cities like York, Richmond, Sydney, and Madrid, and currently resides in a secret hideaway somewhere in the swamps of Florida where he continues to grow his collection of colors.

ALSO BY JOHN URBANCIK

COLLECTIONS

Shadows, Legends & Secrets
Sound and Vision
Tales of the Fantastic and the Phantasmagoric
The Museum of Curiosities

POETRY

John the Revelator
Odyssey
Annabel Lee, In Shadow
The Ruins of Love

NOVELLAS

A Game of Colors
The Rise and Fall of Babylon (with Brian Keene)
Wings of the Butterfly
House of Shadow and Ash
Necropolis
Quicksilver
Beneath Midnight
Zombies vs. Aliens vs. Robots vs. Cowboys vs.
Ninja vs. Investment Bankers vs. Green Berets
Colette and the Tiger
Madmen, Poets & Thieves
Clockwork Ravens
The Night Carnival
La Casa del Diablo

ALSO BY JOHN URBANCIK

NOVELS

Sins of Blood and Stone
Breath of the Moon
Once Upon a Time in Midnight
Stale Reality
The Corpse and the Girl from Miami
DarkWalker 1: Hunting Grounds
DarkWalker 2: Inferno
DarkWalker 3: The Deep City
DarkWalker 4: Armageddon
DarkWalker 5: Ghost Stories
DarkWalker 6: Other Realms
Choose Your Doom
Army of Blood and Stone

NONFICTION

InkStained: On Creativity, Writing, and Art

MEMOIR

Urbancik

INKSTAINS

Multiple volumes

www.ingramcontent.com/pod-product-compliance
Lightning Source LLC
LaVergne TN
LVHW051011080826
845145LV00009B/2568

* 9 7 8 1 9 5 1 5 2 2 2 4 7 *